Technical Analysis

A Newbies' Guide

An Everyday Guide to Technical Analysis of the Financial Markets

Alan Northcott

www.alannorthcott.com

www.newbiesguidetotechnicalanalysis.com

Copyright Notice

First Printing, 2014

ISBN-13: 978-1497329379

ISBN-10: 149732937X

Printed in the United States of America

Disclaimer and Risk Disclosure

By reading this book you agree that this book and any ideas expressed within are for informational and educational purposes only and do not constitute advice or recommendations. Trading in the financial markets, whether for short or long-term purposes, is risky and may not be suitable for all investors. You must understand that you may lose any money invested.

Before you start share trading, you should carefully consider your financial situation, your level of experience and knowledge, and your appetite for risk. You could lose some or all of your trading capital, and you must understand how to mitigate that risk. No liability is accepted by Alan Northcott or his successors for any losses whether direct, indirect or consequential suffered by the use of any information contained herein.

The information given in this book is for educational and personal enjoyment purposes only, and is not a recommendation to enter into trading in any form. If any specific trading or investment or legal advice is required, the services of a competent and appropriately licensed person should be sought.

TABLE OF CONTENTS

Introduction

What is technical analysis? Is it something for the nerd to revel in and a regular person to be perplexed about?

No, it is actually something that is very simple in concept, but can be plumbed to great depths. Let us first get something out of the way. The "technical" in technical analysis does not mean that you have to be an "A" student in mathematics to be able to understand and use it.

I have an engineering background and a mathematical bent. That is probably not surprising. My mother worked in the tax office, would amuse herself on bus journeys by making up number puzzles with the serial number of the bus ticket, and would always know exactly how much the bill should be at the local supermarket by the time she got to the checkout.

It helped that in England they do not add tax to the total but include it in the article pricing; but to make it harder, those were the days of pounds, shillings, and pence, so no easy decimal addition.

My father was in banking all his life, and was a foreign-exchange manager. So you can see that the left side of my brain was bound to be dominant in my life.

When it came to trading the markets, I naturally thought that I had a built in advantage. I was wrong. Technical analysis is as much an art as a science, and you cannot just formally calculate the inevitable winners. No one can.

What you can do is increase your odds of success. With the markets, much as some may tell you this or that "will happen" if you see a certain signal, nothing is inevitable. At best, the signal means more likely than not.

By increasing your odds of success, on average you will choose better and stand to make a decent profit from your trading.

Once you accept that you cannot "know" definitively which way the market is going, but only tip the probabilities in your favor, then you may still be worried that "technical" means you have some calculations to perform.

Do not be concerned. Computers and software do all the hard work for a regular trader, and provide all the information you need with no mathematical ability necessary. I talk in the book about the calculations that make up the trading indicators you may use simply so you can understand why they work. You will not even need a calculator to use them.

A.N.

P.S. If you become interested in the more intuitive side of trading, I recommend a book by Curtis Faith, one of the original Turtle Traders, called *"Trading From Your Gut"*. I wrote an endorsement for it, but do not benefit from recommending it.

P.P.S. Although it is a fascinating read, if you are a Newbie I would recommend you getting familiar with conventional technical analysis first before trying out the methods of Curtis's book.

The Dow Theory

Typically, a discussion of technical analysis must start with the Dow Theory. Charles Dow was one of the fathers of modern trading, and his name is still remembered today in the Dow Jones Industrial Average, one of the leading stock market indices that is often simply called the "Dow".

Dow teamed up with Edward Jones in 1882, forming a business that delivered a handwritten newsletter to banks and brokerages. This became known as the Wall Street Journal in 1889, and is still in publication.

Dow wrote many articles about the markets, which always fascinated him, and he decided to put together an average of stock values in 1884. To Dow, this provided a ready means to indicate the health of business.

The first average was made up of 11 stocks, nine of which were railroad stocks. In 1896, Dow decided to split out the transportation stocks into a separate index, and that is when the Dow Jones

Industrial Average (DJIA) and the Dow Jones Transportation Average (DJTA) came into being.

The new DJIA included 12 stocks and the DJTA had 20. Dow had shown exceptional insight by recognizing the importance of tracking individual market sectors.

Dow wrote a lot about his thoughts on the stock market, mainly in the form of editorials published in the Wall Street Journal. He died in 1902. He never wrote a book, and the term "Dow Theory" was coined after his death when his notes were assembled.

Dow's Principles

It is said that Dow never saw his observations as a means to trade the stock market, but simply a way of describing general economic prosperity. Nonetheless, the principles that he voiced are still considered valid and applicable to trading. They are usually spelled out as six tenets or principles: –

1. The averages reflect everything that can be known about a price.
2. The markets exhibit three types of price movement.
3. Primary movements have three phases.
4. It takes both the DJIA and the DJTA to confirm a trend.
5. Volume must increase in the direction of the trend to confirm it.

6. A trend continues until there is a clear reversal.

1. Averages Reflect Everything

The first principle leads to one of the fundamental beliefs of technical analysis, that the market discounts everything. In other words, the action of the market reflects everything there is to know about a price.

Dow was speaking about averages, because that was his focus, but nowadays this principle is applied to individual prices. It seems simplistic, but turns out to be one of the fundamental concepts validating technical analysis.

If you think about it, there are many things that can affect the price of a stock or commodity. Sales are obviously important, as are costs, industrial unrest, government legislation, and the price of raw materials; and the list goes on.

The idea that the "market discounts everything" allows the technical analyst to ignore each of these individual factors, and cut to the bottom line. After all, it does not matter which element is changing, supply and demand control the price, and the outcome is all that the analyst is concerned with.

This makes the job of the analyst much simpler, indeed it makes it manageable. The reason the price is moving is not important, you simply need to be able to discern that it is, and in what direction.

2. Three Types of Movement

Dow identified three types of market movement:-

- a primary movement or trend, which lasts for a year or more;
- a secondary movement, which may take three weeks to three months and is basically a retracement or a taking back of some of the primary movement;
- and a tertiary movement, which is basically a fluctuation in price that lasts less than three weeks.

Bear in mind that Dow was concerned with major or fundamental changes in value, rather than the short-term fluctuations that traders usually look for. Traders can certainly use trends, but the natural cyclical action of the markets they look for is usually on a shorter timescale.

3. Three Phases

The three phases of Dow Theory arise from human psychology, and are as evident today as they were in Dow's time.

Considering an uptrend, that is a "bull" market, the first phase is called the "accumulation phase". That is when a trend starts, and the smartest or luckiest investors have figured out that the stock is a good buy and increasing in value.

The second phase is usually the longest, and that happens when other buyers have noticed the rising price and decide to buy into the trend. The volume of trading goes up as many others jump on the shares, so this is called the "public participation phase".

After time, jumping on the trend becomes no more than speculation, and based on hope rather than true worth. The initial investors usually drop out and take their profits here. This phase is called the "distribution phase".

Simply looking at a price chart, you cannot really tell which phase a trend is in, but using technical analysis you can pick up some clues. You obviously want to buy as soon as a reliable trend is started, though if it is the first or second phase does not really matter. It is good to avoid buying in the distribution phase, as it becomes increasingly likely that the price will stop rising, and may even start to fall.

4. Both DJIA and DJTA to Confirm

Dow always considered that both of these indexes had to be moving in the same direction to confirm a trend, whether up or down. He would not believe in a trend until they were moving together, and considered the trend continuing until both reversed.

This is based on sound logic. If manufacturing is up, as indicated by a rise in the Industrial Average, then there is more transportation required and the Transportation Average should be increasing too. Anything else suggests an unstable situation. This idea is often summed up in the expression "what one makes, the other takes."

5. Volume Increasing to Confirm

Dow realized the importance of trading volume in confirming the strength of a trend. If you like, volume is a vote on whether the price is going in the right direction. If there is little trading, or few "votes", then you do not really know the will of the majority of the market, and could be caught out.

6. Trends Tend to Continue

Without a good reason, trends tend to keep going in the same direction. You can see this by looking at the price charts, which some of the time seem to go up and down randomly, presumably when the price is about right, but exhibit clear direction when in a trend.

For a physical comparison, simply consider Newton's Laws of Motion, which state that an object will keep moving unless acted upon by an external force. There is usually a discernible reason why trends come to an end.

Those six points are considered to be the basis for modern trading theories, even though Dow was not strictly a trader but looked at the long-term outcome. The fundamentals of Technical Analysis are usually summarized in the following three beliefs.

The Market Discounts Everything

As mentioned under Dow's first tenet, this principle allows technical analysis to happen without needing unbelievable complication. You are simply interested in what the market shows you is happening to the price and traders' enthusiasm, and you really do not care what has caused that action.

The corollary of this is that you must let the market tell you where it is going, and not assume that it will go where it "should," according to logic or your feelings. If you try to fight the market, you will end up the loser.

The Market Exhibits Trends

Trends are mentioned in several of Dow's tenets. The last one is the most important to us; simply that a trend tends to keep on going unless there is a reason for it to stop. The reason for stopping may simply be that it has got to as high (or as low) a level as all the various factors dictate it should, in other words the trend may run out of steam; technical analysis has tools to give you a clue if this is happening.

Many traders use "trend following" strategies, which involve identifying a trend as quickly as possible, trading with it, and then exiting the position before the trend fails.

The opposite "countertrend" type of strategies are usually more difficult to work. In essence, they involve trying to judge when a trend is ceasing so that you can trade in the opposite direction by identifying a point of reversal.

History Repeats Itself

Over and over again! This third fundamental simply says that what happened in the past is likely to happen again now and in the future, when the same circumstances come about.

People do not change, and the psychology of the markets, with all the conflicting emotions that they cause, is such that you can reasonably expect the same outcome a lot of the time.

Remember, the philosopher George Santayana said in 1924 "those who cannot remember the past are condemned to repeat it," which works in our favor when we are trying to anticipate what will happen next. We rely on a study of history, in the shape of previous market action, to help us foresee the future.

Basic Charting

Technical analysis is based on two sets of numbers. The first and most obvious set, and the one that most people think of, is the price and the way it varies over time. If you have ever looked at stock market charts, you will be familiar with the layout, with time running along the bottom and price going up the side.

Line Charts

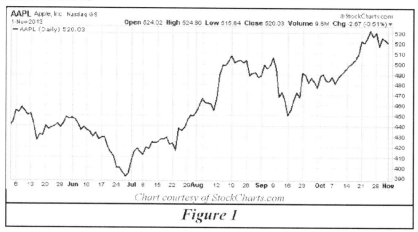

Figure 1

All the charts in this book are courtesy of **StockCharts.com**, and I encourage you to explore their website as you can find most things that you will need to practice with freely available there. I have also copied these charts to the book's website, **www.newbiesguidetotechnicalanalysis**, for clarity.

This is the chart of Apple, Inc., share price for the six months from May to October 2013. The dates are shown along the bottom, and the price levels from $390 to $530 are on the right. The thick line shows the way the price has changed from a starting level of about $440 to about $520 over time.

You can see that the line is far from smooth. It does not show every little price fluctuation on this scale, but just one value, the price when the market closed on each weekday, and it has gone up and down a lot, or been "volatile" as it is called.

By the way, any chart that shows daily values, like this, will only have five days or values in a week and not seven, as prices do not change when the markets are not open so those days are not plotted.

This is a basic price chart, and is called a line chart because the price values are connected by a line. It tells you a lot, even though it only shows one value for each day. Although technical analysis considers only price and volume of trading and disregards any fundamental data, we have easy access to much more price information than is shown here.

When the markets open, the first trade that happens is at the "opening price", which may be at a greater or lesser value than trading that happened on the previous day. The trading goes on during the day, with the price moving up and down, and the last trade that happens on the day is at the "closing price".

We know even more than this from the day's trading. Because the price has gone up and down, we can also identify the highest and lowest prices at which the stock has traded at any time during the day.

This means we have four price values for each day. Certainly, on some days prices may not be different – for instance the stock price at the open may be the lowest it trades at all day long, making the open and the low price the same – but this is a lot more information than the single value for each day.

Bar Charts

Up until 20 or 30 years ago, Western traders would learn to use something called "bar charts" or "OHLC charts" (standing for open-high-low-close). This is the way that all four prices can be represented on a chart for each day.

Each day's trading is represented by a vertical line which runs from the lowest price level to the highest price level. It allows you to easily see the range of prices which have occurred in trading.

In addition, the opening price is shown by a short horizontal line, named a "tic", sticking out to the left of the vertical bar, and the closing price is represented by another tic which sticks out to the right. Here is a visual representation much magnified of one day's trade, one bar.

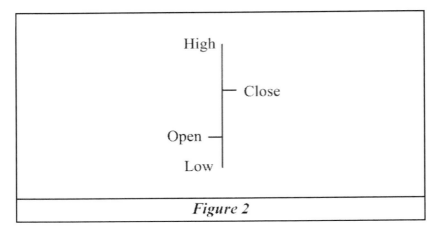

Figure 2

Each day is represented by one bar, so the Apple chart which we looked at previously would look like this: –

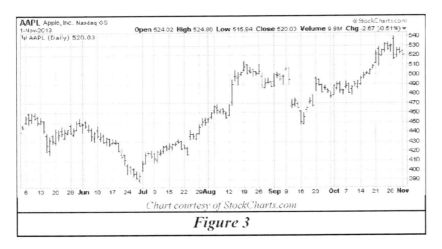

Chart courtesy of StockCharts.com

Figure 3

16

Scaled down to fit the book this may be difficult to read; if so look at the chart online or see the original on the website.

Even on this scale, you can see some interesting things that the bar chart shows you that the line chart does not, such as some gaps in pricing, including a big drop in the early part of September.

Candlestick Charts

The bar chart served the Western trader for many years, but thanks to a guy called Steve Nison we now have a system showing the four prices which is much clearer and easier to discern.

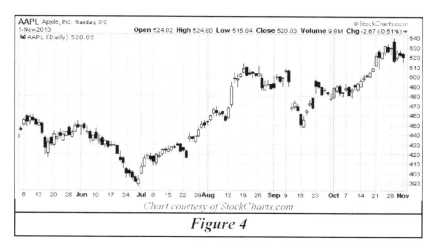

Figure 4

Figure 4 shows a candlestick chart for the same security. Steve Nison is a Western trader who is known as the "father of candlestick charting", having brought the idea from Japan in 1989. Candlesticks or candlecharts have been used in

Japan for centuries, but for some reason had never been discovered by Western traders.

The most obvious difference is that part of each vertical line or bar now has a thickness, and is either white or black. If you know nothing more, you can see that the chart stands out better than the bar chart.

The way the candlestick symbol is drawn is that the vertical line or bar still goes between the lowest and highest prices for the day, but there is a solid body between the opening price and closing price. The body is one color if the opening price is higher than the closing price, and another if vice versa.

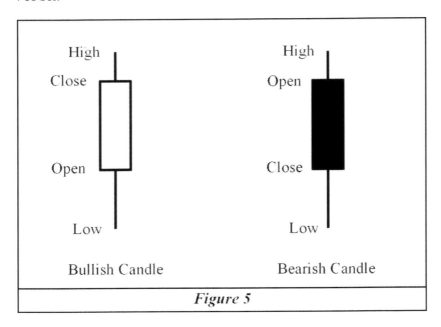

Figure 5

Remember that bullish means overall the prices are rising, and bearish means that they are falling.

In these black-and-white charts the body is white if the opening price is lower than the closing price, that is the price is going up, and is black if the price is going down, with the opening price greater than the closing price. Most charting software allows you to choose the colors, so you may see green when the price is going up and red when it goes down, for instance.

The solid part, whether black or white, is called the "real body". The lines going up and down from the real body are called "shadows" or "wicks", in line with the image of this symbol looking like a candle.

There can be many variations in the overall look of the candle, depending on the price values. The body can be long or short, or even just a horizontal line (very short), the wicks can be long, short, or nonexistent, and all these factors are interpreted in terms of market sentiment, or how traders are viewing the price of the stock.

There is a lot more to learn about candlestick charts, so I cover them in a later chapter. For now, it is enough to see that even though they show exactly the same amount of information, they are clearer to use than bar charts. For this reason, I mainly use candlestick charts in the rest of the book.

Charting Volume

I mentioned at the beginning of this chapter that technical analysis is based on two sets of numbers, with prices being the first. Associated with each trade or price there is also a volume, for example how many shares are traded at that price. The volume of trading is available generally on a daily basis, and it shows how many shares changed hands on a trading day. The volume is usually shown as a bar chart, either superimposed on the bottom of the price chart or shown separately under, as below in Figure 6.

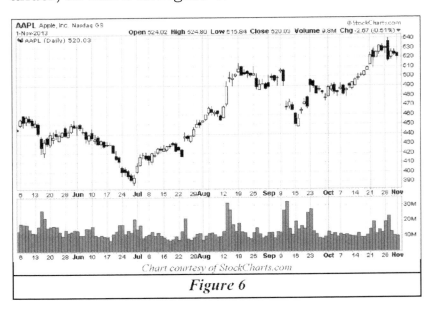

Chart courtesy of StockCharts.com

Figure 6

You will see in a later chapter that the volume of trading can be every bit as important as the price, so you should not neglect to include consideration of it in your technical analysis.

The basic principle when considering volume is that, if there is not much trading, then the price movement is not a reliable indication of the market sentiment as a whole. If there is a large volume on any particular day, then that counts almost as a "vote" in favor of the way the price behaved and the level it reached, so you can trust it more.

Finally, for this chapter I have for convenience only shown daily charts, as this is probably the most popular timeframe. You can get charts with many different periods along the bottom, whether it is long range charts with weeks or months for each candlestick, or day trading charts where you might see a candlestick added every few minutes – 5 minutes, 30 minutes, an hour are some of the time periods used.

Technical analysis principles apply to all different timeframes, and the analysis is similar. You will find that it is a good idea to look at several timeframes to get a better picture of the behavior of any particular stock price.

I use stocks for the examples in this book, but technical analysis applies to all manner of trading – futures markets, Forex, etc. Technical analysis is based on human psychology, and this is constant regardless of the financial instrument being traded.

What is a Trend?

The idea of a price having a trend or not is a basic one in technical analysis. Earlier, I pointed out that often we can expect prices to continue in the direction they are going, in other words maintaining a trend, so it helps our trading if we can be more sure when and if a trend exists.

I would also point out that prices do not follow trends all the time, in fact some analysts say that 40% of the time prices tend to float around the same level, with no particular direction. This is called "trendless" price behavior, or sometimes "range bound" or range trading. The exact amount of trendless activity would depend on many factors, including the markets traded, economic outlook, etc. It is enough to know that it is significant, and you cannot always expect to find a definite trend.

Most people think they can recognize a trend just from glancing at a chart. After all, it is pretty obvious if the price line is sloping up or down showing trending activity, or hanging around the same price level.

The trouble with this informal approach is that it may not be reliable. What one person thinks is a trend may be seen by another as simply the price floating up within a limited price range, likely to drift down again. More importantly, whether the price line looks like a trend may depend on the timescale that you are using. This can be a problem, even when you try to apply a more formal definition to a trend. Here is the Apple price chart again: -

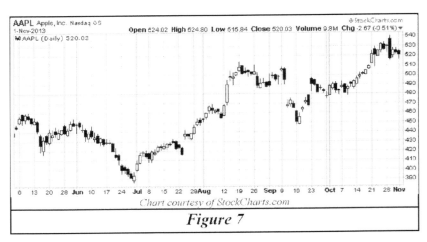

Figure 7

Looking from the middle of September to today you might think that there is a clear uptrend. That is true on this scale, but if you were to look at the beginning of October you can see that there were several days when the price fell steadily, so a chart which only considered a few days, perhaps based on hourly candlesticks, would have convinced you that there was a strong downtrend instead.

You can see there are several more examples of this phenomenon on the chart. It is the nature of prices not to go straight up or down, but to have "consolidation" or "retracement" areas when the price hesitates or moves countertrend.

When you are analyzing charts, and looking for patterns that might be repeated, you want to have a consistent method of defining the various attributes, such as a trend. So technical analysts came up with a definition by which you could decide whether or not a trend existed.

The definition is simple. An uptrend has successively higher peaks and higher troughs as shown in Figure 8, and a downtrend has successively lower peaks and troughs (figure 9 over).

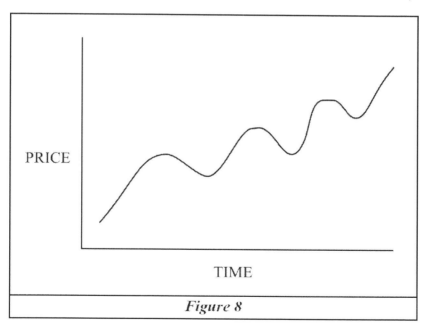

PRICE

TIME

Figure 8

This means for an uptrend to be shown, whenever the fluctuations take the price down it never goes lower than a previous low point. If it did, then the trend would be considered flawed and possibly failing.

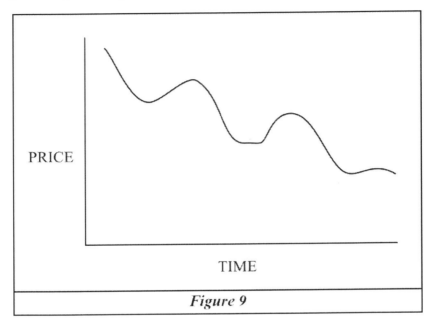

PRICE

TIME

Figure 9

Figure 9 shows a simplified downtrend. In this case, the price must never rise as high as the previous peak for the trend to be considered valid.

You can see that this method is still subject to possible problems, as it does not resolve likely conflicts between different time scales of chart. Usually the analyst will simply look at the main timescale that his trading strategy uses, and determine whether it is a trend from that. After all, if he is trading on that timeframe, that is the timeframe of the price performance he is interested in.

Looking at these simplified charts, you can relate them back to the Dow Theory. He spoke of the primary movement and the secondary movement in price, and that is what is shown here. On a more detailed level, you would also see the tertiary movement of the price, again more "jiggles" in the chart.

Support and Resistance

Just as the concept of a trend is fundamental to technical analysis, so is the idea of "support and resistance". Actually, there are two types of support and resistance, one using fixed levels and the other using levels that change as a trend advances.

First, support is a price level below which you do not expect the price to go. The price may come down and touch the level, but then it will go back up again. The level therefore provides support for the stock price.

For now, just accept this idea. I will show you many examples which demonstrate how it works in practice, and also discuss one theoretical way why it should be so.

Resistance is similar, but provides a cap on how high a price can go before it drops back down. The price may go soaring up, but it runs into resistance and is turned away.

27

Looking back at the simple diagrams above, you can picture how in an uptrend the price runs into resistance and falls back; as it goes down it hits a support and starts going up again. You can apply the same kind of analysis to the downtrend diagram.

Does this mean we can predict in advance where the support and resistance levels will be, and therefore have a much clearer picture of how the price will change? If you could know when the price is going to fluctuate, it would certainly help in being a successful trader.

The answer is to this is "yes and no". We can use technical analysis to give us a fair idea of where the price will run into support and resistance, in some cases. It is one of the tools that traders use regularly.

I mentioned above that there are two types of support and resistance. First, carrying on from the previous discussion of a trend, we will look at the support and resistance lines that are angled with a trend. Another word describing these is trendlines.

In an uptrend, when prices are increasing, the primary trendline is a support line, a straight line that slopes up drawn underneath all the prices. It only takes two points to draw a straight line, so you can make one as soon as you have two clear low points in an uptrend.

At this stage, the trendline is only tentative, just a trial that you will look at in future to see if it is holding. The trendline starts to be significant if you have the price coming down and touching it a third time before going back up.

Of course, a trendline is not exact, and there is discussion on whether you should connect the lowest points of the wicks or the real bodies, but you can see the idea play out in this chart of E*Trade share prices.

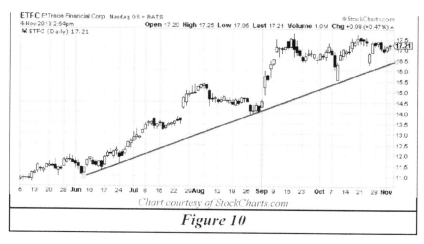

Figure 10

Back in June, there were two or three low points that could be connected. The share price took off, but came back to the same trendline in September, and found support for another surge. It visited again in the middle of October, and almost came down to touch a couple of weeks later.

In practice, you probably would not have had any conclusions from the start in June, as the price

29

then stayed well above the trendline. But once it hit and rebounded in September, you could draw the line with more confidence, and almost expect the reversals in October.

This chart is also a good example of what you may find in practice. You will seldom see the price behaving well, as in the simplified diagrams, but you will need to take a view on the underlying values, and learn to rule out the "noise".

Considering a downtrend, the trendline is drawn connecting the high points as they come down, creating a resistance level that you do not expect the price to rise above. Here is one drawn on Cisco Systems.

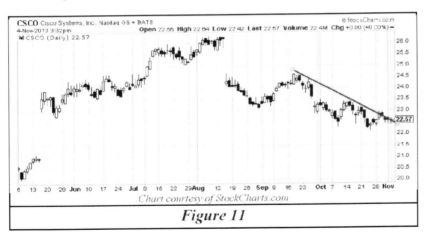

Chart courtesy of StockCharts.com

Figure 11

Once again, an imperfect example, and it shows you the principle. The trendline could have been started before October, but did not have any authority until mid-October when twice it stopped the price rising higher. On the far right you can see

30

that the trendline has been broken, but only just – you would have to look to other indicators to see if you should expect the price to continue to fall, or if this marks a possible change in the trend.

The other type of support and resistance lines are lines that are drawn horizontally on the chart at certain price levels. As you would expect, these are less likely to be useful when a price is trending, but can often, perhaps even months later, provide the support or resistance for a price that returns to the range.

Because these lines are drawn horizontally, you can draw them as soon as you have one low point (for a support line) or one high point (for a resistance line).

Support and resistance values are levels that appear difficult for the price to cross, and that applies whichever direction the price comes from. In other words, a line which presented resistance to the price going up once the price has broken it may provide support to the price coming back down, and vice versa.

Figure 12 overleaf is a chart for 3D Systems Corporation.

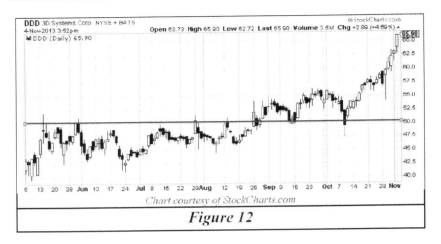

Figure 12

You can see that the 50 price level presented resistance across the left half of the chart. After the price passed through it, it then became a support level twice on the right-hand side.

This raises another point about support and resistance levels. Often you will find that they are at notable whole number levels, in this case 50. You may see them for example at 10, 20, 100, and other numbers like that.

On the one hand, it might seem strange that the price should get stuck at numbers which appear significant to us. However, if you think about it, it is not so strange. Virtually all price movements are governed by human psychology, which obviously places significance on these levels.

Assessing Strength

You may be wondering how you can determine when to trust and rely on support and resistance levels. In the long run, they may all be broken, but for trading purposes you would like to know how much you can expect them to work.

There are a couple of general principles that help you with this assessment.

Firstly, if the level has been approached several times by the price, but the price has moved away, in other words the line has been tested, then the level will be more reliable than a single touch and retreat. Coincidentally, this also makes it more easy to determine the support or resistance level in the first place.

Secondly, you should look at how long the price has been trading up to the resistance or down to the support level. If it has been doing so for several months, this too means that the level can be thought more reliable.

Why It Works

I promised at the start of this section to discuss one reason why support and resistance could logically work. It may not be wholly accurate, but it is a useful way to think about the psychology and mechanics of trading.

Think of the people who are in the market as being divided into three groups. The first group has already bought the stock, the second group has taken a "short" position, that is a trade which profits when the price goes down, and the third group is currently standing to one side, watching the stock but not making any trades yet.

Say the stock price is rising off a support level. The people in the first group are happy, and perhaps even thinking they should have bought more of the stock. In contrast, the people in the second group are unhappy, and hoping the price will come back down so that they can exit the short trade at about the same price as they entered, minimizing their losses. The third group, if they are still watching the stock, may be wishing that they had bought some at the original price, cannot see buying it now the price has gone up, but might be interested if the price came back down to the original level.

Can you see what would happen if the price comes back down to the support level? The first group would eagerly buy some more stock, the second group would close their short positions, effectively buying the stock, and the third group would decide to buy the stock and not miss out this time. So all the market participants would want to buy at the support level, and the demand would make the price go back up, "proving" the support.

So much for what makes a support work. I suggest you go through the exercise, considering why the resistance level works, in the same manner. This simple breakdown of the psychology can even provide us with a reason why the support can become resistance, and vice versa.

Think about what happens if the price actually falls through the support level, and keeps on going. Everyone's thought processes will have to change.

The first group are now unhappy, thinking they have made a mistake buying the stock. They might choose to hang on to see if the price comes back up to the support level, just so they do not lose too much when they sell. The second group who shorted the stock are very happy as it looks as though they got it right. They could be thinking that if the price came back up to the support level, they should take the opportunity to short some more shares. And the third group of undecided traders might see this as an indication that they should have taken a short position, and resolve to do that if only the price would come back up to the support level.

The result of all this thinking is that all three groups decide to sell if the price comes back up to the support level. By the law of supply and demand, with so much supply the price will drop, fulfilling the change of function of the level to a resistance.

Both forms of support and resistance, the horizontal ones and the trendline ones, are important when you are setting targets and limits for your trading. They are one of the simplest ways to determine specific levels that you may expect to see, and help you work out your reward v. possible risk.

Chart Patterns

In this chapter, we will look at some of the common patterns or shapes that the price chart can exhibit. For many years these were the only patterns that traders looked for. When candlestick charting was introduced to the West, another family of chart patterns came with it, and we will consider those in a later chapter.

As with all technical analysis, but particularly in this case, what constitutes a pattern is a subjective judgment. You just have to work on the best information available, interpreting it as earnestly as you can. Even then, the initial warning that analysis only indicates the balance of probability of what will happen still applies. With all that said, patterns can be useful in indicating future expectations, and in identifying critical price levels.

Patterns are usually broken down into two types, reversal patterns and continuation patterns. Reversal patterns predominate, as they may alert you to a change in trend that is coming, a useful warning from a trading perspective. Continuation patterns, as the name suggests, simply mean that the trend will continue, so are less exciting. After all, the trend continuing is one of the basic ideas of technical analysis, so this is a case of "no news". Still, they can reassure you that the trend does not seem to be weakening.

Reversal Patterns

Head-and-Shoulders

One of the most well known patterns in the trading community, the head-and-shoulders and its variants often appear in uptrends, signaling an end to the trend and possible reversal. This pattern gets its name from the fact that it consists of three price peaks, with the middle one slightly higher than either side. The middle is the "head", and each side is a "shoulder". Here is an idealized representation:

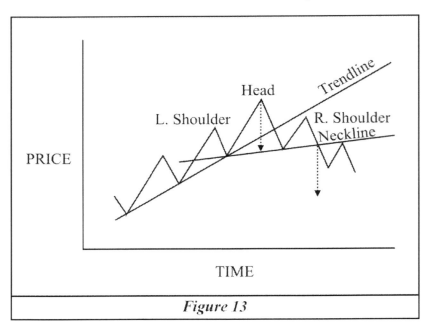

Figure 13

This pattern occurs in an uptrend, and shows a weakening of the trend and a reversal into a downtrend. To help you see the original trend, there is a trend line sloping up from left to right, and initially the price is taking this as a support.

However, once the price has reached the level of the "Head" it declines and drops through the support of the trendline, giving the first indication that the trend may be over. Even then, the price might have stopped at the same level as the left shoulder, taking this as a horizontal support level.

There is a weak rally in price which forms the right shoulder, and as this does not reach as high as the head level the trend appears to be over, which is proved by subsequent events. You will usually see the volume of trading reduce also as the pattern progresses, another indication of lessening enthusiasm for the stock. Volume is covered in more depth in the next chapter.

Note that a line connecting the low points either side of the head is called the neckline, and may provide resistance to subsequent price movements. It often slopes slightly upwards as shown, but can be horizontal or sloping downward. The pattern is considered validated once the price has dropped below the neckline.

The dotted arrows are added to show you one way that you can set targets for your trading. The arrows are both the same length, and the distance from the head down to the neckline represents the minimum amount you can expect the price to fall below the neckline, once the reversal is confirmed.

As you can see, there is no particular "magic" to this pattern. The way the price goes simply describes a weakening and reversing of a trend. Still, it gives you a shape to look for as you glance through the charts, looking for a tradable stock.

Many other reversal patterns are based on this simple concept of the head-and-shoulders pattern. For example, if you start with a downtrend you may see an "Inverse Head-and-Shoulders" pattern, which is basically the same pattern upside down and turns into an uptrend.

Other variants include the "Complex Head-and-Shoulders Pattern". As the name suggests, this is a more complicated pattern than the basic one, and it includes extra parts, such as two heads or a double shoulder. In effect the same trend reversal is occurring, but taking more time to resolve.

The Head-and-Shoulders can fail, even when the price has dropped below the neckline. The first sign that it is not going to result in a reversal may be if the price goes back over the neckline, and you may even find that the original uptrend resumes. Trading and technical analysis is a percentage game and not an exact science, therefore sometimes you will see the unexpected.

Triple Top and Bottom

The Triple Top reversal pattern is very similar to the head-and-shoulders, but with the head at a similar level to the other two peaks. It is much rarer to find this than the conventional head-and-shoulders, but if you see it the analysis is essentially the same.

It shows a general weakening in the uptrend, and you should find that the volume of trading is less for each successive peak. In contrast, the volume may increase on the downward slopes, in essence emphasizing the mood of the market to reverse.

In a similar way, the Triple Bottom reversal pattern is like the Inverse Head and Shoulders and may appear in a downtrend, signaling a possible change to an uptrend.

Double Top and Bottom

Another similar formation is the double pattern, which is almost as common as the head-and-shoulders. The Double Top can also be referred to as the "M" top simply because of the way it looks. It consists of two peaks at roughly the same level, and after the second peak the price drops below the low point between them.

Once again the analysis is similar, and it is important to see that the volume of trading is less going up to the second peak than the first, and quite possibly more on the downward slope, as this will help confirm that the market sentiment.

The Double Bottom can be called the "W" bottom, and occurs after a downtrend as a reversal into an uptrend. Once again, you can look for the price levels and volumes that would provide confirmation of the likely reversal.

One of the dangers when looking for Double Tops and Bottoms is that you will see many price movements that can be mistaken for them. Just consider how support and resistance levels work to limit the price from going further than the previous one. You might simply find that the price is going to fluctuate in a trendless way between support and resistance levels. This is sometimes also called range trading, as the price stays in a fixed range.

You can check on this by making sure that the price drops below the previous low point in the next down move. This gives you the best chance of it being a genuine reversal.

Reversal patterns must always follow a trend. If there is no trend beforehand, then there is no specific meaning to the shape of the price line. The importance of the pattern is usually indicated by the size of the pattern, with a larger pattern being more significant. For instance, most double patterns have at least a month between peaks.

Continuation Patterns

Continuation patterns are usually of a shorter duration than reversal patterns. They tend to happen during periods of consolidation before a trend continues. Once again, if you see one of these patterns it does not mean that the trend must continue, but on the balance of probabilities where it has been seen before, that is what happens.

Triangles

There are several different forms of triangle pattern, and they often result in a continuation of a trend. As with reversals, you need to have the price in a trend for the interpretation to make any sense.

Most triangle patterns you will be looking for start out big and get smaller over time, forming the triangle shape. In the following diagrams I have continued the price line after it has broken out of the triangle shape, and shown it going in the direction which it will normally take. As you will see, for each of these examples it is shown as a continuation of the trend in place when the triangle started.

The markets will often surprise you, so sometimes the price will take off in the other direction after leaving the triangle, but that is much less likely.

Symmetrical Triangle

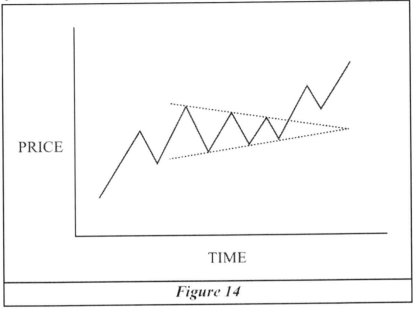

Figure 14

Taking first the symmetrical triangle, Figure 14 above, as you can see this is a relatively neutral shape to up or down, and you will see it in either uptrends or downtrends. It usually provides a pausing place before the trend continues. You can see it forming once you have two high points and two low points, when you can draw the trendlines that will intercept at the apex of the triangle. Often it will continue as shown, being constrained by the triangle three times on the top and on the bottom before it breaks out.

You can see from the pattern that it is forced to resolve in one direction or the other within a finite period of time – the price is getting squeezed into a smaller and smaller space. You may notice the trading volume reducing during the formation of the triangle, with heavier volume once the breakout resolves.

Ascending Triangle

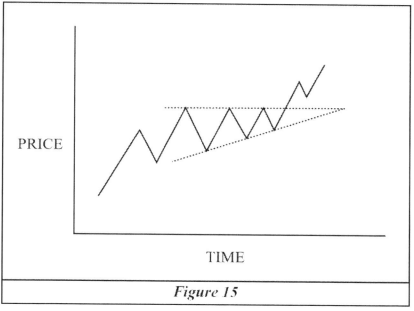

Figure 15

Looking next at the ascending triangle in Figure 15, you can see it is shown in an uptrend, and is distinguished by the top line being horizontal.

Unlike the symmetrical triangle, this pattern is definitely bullish, and may even occur in a downtrend, when it is taken to signal a reversal into an uptrend.

The interpretation is that buyers are determinedly trading up to a resistance level, and that eventually the resistance fails and the price breaks out.

Descending Triangle

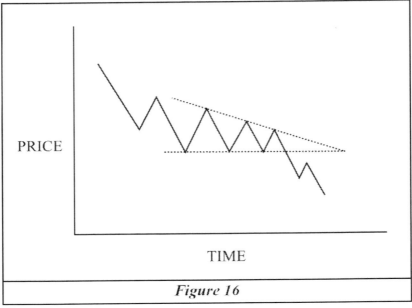

PRICE

TIME

Figure 16

You can apply exactly the same type of reasoning to the descending triangle shown above, which has a horizontal bottom line or support level and is usually bearish.

All these triangles will tend to take about a month before they resolve.

You may be wondering if you can have a triangle the other way, with larger fluctuations over time. The answer is yes you can, and it usually means you should watch out because the market is acting very erratically.

Broadening Formation

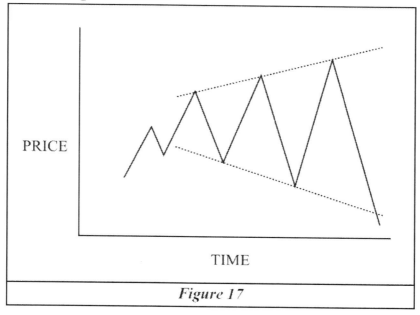

Figure 17

This is called a broadening formation, and it is really anyone's guess what direction the price will finally go in. Usually the volume of trading is increasing over time, forcing the price harder and harder against the upper and lower lines until something has to give way.

The Flag

There are also some shorter term signals of a continuation. The "flag" shown in Figure 18 below may take a couple of weeks to complete.

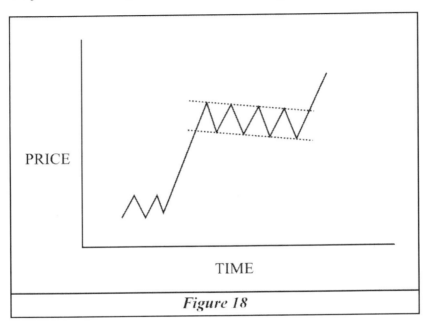

PRICE

TIME

Figure 18

It often follows a sharp increase in price, as shown, and seems to provide a pause to the market before the surge continues. You can also find it the other way round, in a downtrend, when it would tend to point upwards – the flag usually slopes against the trend.

The Pennant

The "pennant" is similar in interpretation, providing a pause to the price increase.

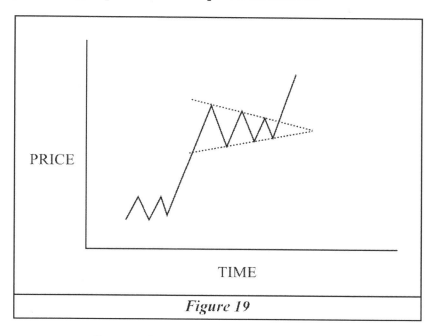

Figure 19

At first sight you might think it is a symmetrical triangle. The difference is that it comes after a steep rise or fall in price, and it lasts a much shorter time.

The Rectangle

The rectangle goes by several names – Charles Dow called it a "line" – and it is another type of consolidation period during a trend, which usually results in the trend continuing. For example, in an uptrend it looks like this: –

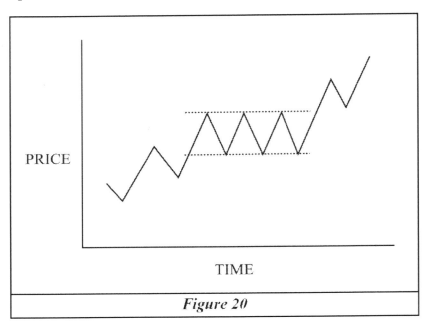

Figure 20

You can get clues from the volume of trading whether the price will continue upwards or not. It is a good idea to check the volumes, as otherwise you could get this confused with the triple top which is a reversal pattern.

The rectangle is really just a way of describing range trading or sideways trading between a support and a resistance level, and the expectation that at some stage one or other will be broken, allowing a trading opportunity.

Head-and-Shoulders

For the sake of completeness, I should mention that the head-and-shoulders pattern can also be seen as a continuation pattern. In this case it would come in a downtrend, and signify a likely continuation of the downtrend. In other words, whether in an uptrend, where it would be a reversal signal, or in a downtrend, where it is continuation signal, the head-and-shoulders pattern tends to resolve into a downtrend.

Similarly, you will sometimes see the inverse head and shoulders pattern in an uptrend. The expected result is for the price to continue upwards most often when you see this pattern.

The Importance of Volume

Volume is the number of shares or other financial instruments traded in a certain period of time. Back in the Basic Charting chapter, I gave you an example of how it is usually shown: –

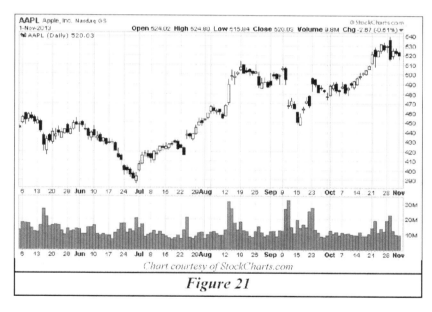

Figure 21

This chart was for Apple Computer over the past six months, with each candlestick representing one day's trading. Below the price chart, there is a vertical bar chart which shows you the number of shares traded on each day. The scale on the right goes up to 30 million, and you can see on a couple of days the amount of trading exceeded this.

There is one primary point to be made about volume – unless volume supports it, any price move (particularly changes in direction) should be viewed with suspicion. Volume is like voting, if it is low then there is not much general support for anything the price does. It is a measure of the enthusiasm that the market participants have for what the price is doing.

So in general you want to see the volume strong and perhaps increasing as a trend develops. On the inevitable retracements in a trend, those times when the price eases back a little before carrying on with the trend, you should see reduced volume. Anything else is a warning sign.

An example of this would be if you see a price going up and making new highs, but each time the volume was dropping. You cannot expect the trend to continue, as you might if you simply looked at the price action.

Technical analysts often say that volume precedes price. In this example the volume is slowing, and you should expect the price to slow or reverse soon.

Going back to the previous pattern chapter, volume can be important in confirming the validity of any of the patterns. For the head and shoulders, the volume will probably get less on each peak, and should increase on the downward price movements. When a pattern resolves, whether as a reversal or a continuation, it is likely that you will see a much heavier volume of trading.

Now to some extent you can determine whether the volume is acting reasonably simply by looking, and indeed some writers suggest that there is no way to substitute a computerized trading indicator for experienced examination of a chart. Anna Coulling in *A Complete Guide to Volume Price Analysis* says that such indicators "have neither the capacity nor intellect to analyze the price volume relationship correctly in my view."

As I said in the introduction, trading is as much an art as a science so I tend to agree with Coulling that an experienced eye can be better than computer indicators. I also recommend her book for more details of the use of volume in trading, particularly as it is bargain priced in the Kindle edition. But following her lead means a novice trader can never get started, or must "invest" a.k.a. squander a great deal of money to pick up the experience needed.

Therefore I believe you should recognize volume characteristics and know about the volume indicators that can point you in the right direction while you are gaining your experience.

On Balance Volume

One of the first volume indicators is called the On Balance Volume (OBV), which was developed about 50 years ago by Granville. It is generally used to confirm a trend, or by showing a divergence from the price can suggest a reversal is imminent.

Before computers became commonplace, this indicator was time intensive, requiring each day's volume to be added or subtracted from a running total. Now it is easily calculated for you by software. Because the start of the running total is arbitrary, the actual value of the OBV is irrelevant, but the direction it moves is important.

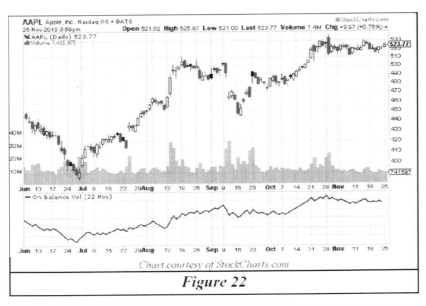

Chart courtesy of StockCharts.com

Figure 22

Note that in this chart I decided to have the volume bar chart superimposed on the bottom of the price chart (the values are on the left) and the OBV positioned underneath.

For the most part, on this chart it seems that the OBV goes in the same direction as the price, so there are no red flags. Possibly you could point out that in the middle of August the price turned down while the OBV kept going upwards, indicating that the downturn was not likely to continue – and indeed it did not until into September, when the OBV turned down too, on heavy trading which is another indication that the market really means it.

The way the OBV is calculated requires that the whole day's trading is added or subtracted from the running total, depending on whether the closing price is above or below the opening. This has the potential problem that a whole lot of volume may be assigned the direction with just a small move in price. Therefore you will find other volume indicators that try and compensate for this in different ways.

If you are interested in exploring the impact of volume on a chart, then I suggest that you invest in Coulling's book, which goes into great detail at minimal expense.

Open Interest

When you are trading stocks or some other financial security, it is clear that you can find out how many stocks were traded in a day. The situation becomes a little more difficult if you are looking at trading futures or options. If you have no interest in commodities, then you can skip this section.

Futures contracts have a different measure of volume, called open interest. Open interest is the total number of contracts that are in existence. As there is a buyer and seller for each contract, there are actually twice as many traders with positions as number of contracts.

Suppose you take out or buy a contract. It names the price and the date for the commodity you have traded. Someone else takes the other side of the contract, believing that the price will go in the opposite direction to the way you expect. One person each side of the contract, and one new contract if you are both new in the market.

As trading continues, you come to a situation where you want to close your contract, for a profit or loss. Because futures are traded on the exchange in an organized manner, it does not matter if the other party to your particular contract wants to close it or not; you can close your contract anyway. The exchange has to match up such orders.

Now it may be that someone else comes along and wants to take your place on the contract, taking the same position that you are giving up. The contract stays the same, it just has a different owner. That means there are still the same number of contracts in existence, even though you liquidated your position.

There is a third possibility. Suppose that you want to liquidate your contract, and someone who has taken the other side to you also wants to liquidate their contract. You are both out of there, and there is one less contract outstanding.

In summary, any time there is a trade in a particular futures contract, it can affect the open interest in one of three ways. The number of contracts can increase, the number can stay the same, or the number can decrease. It just depends whether the person trading was already in the market and getting out, or whether they are taking up a new position.

Even though there is this additional complication, we can still look at the strength or weakness of the market in terms of the open interest. For instance, if open interest is increasing in a rising market, this means that new money is entering into the market, so it is a bullish sign in general.

Take the same rising market but with decreasing open interest, and this shows that the market is weak. The rising price comes mainly from people who are closing their short positions, and once they are all out of their contracts, you can expect the uptrend to slow or reverse.

In a similar way you can look at open interest increasing in a downtrend, which is bearish, and decreasing in a downtrend, which would mean that the traders who are long are closing out their losing positions. Even though this is a downtrend, the sign is bullish suggesting that the slide will slow.

Whenever you look at price movements, you should take into account what the volume is telling you about the sentiment behind those movements. It can reveal a lot more than simply looking at the prices.

Moving Averages

The moving average is an important basic indicator that technical analysts use. It has also been applied in many different ways, and I will cover some of those here. It is the basis of many trading systems.

As an engineer, I had a little difficulty with the way moving averages are shown. After all, when you average a lot of values, you usually show the result in the middle, don't you? Not so with technical analysis. With technical analysis you can average up any number of time periods, as you select, and you put the value on the end, on the current day.

So the average value which you plot is the average of the preceding values. Looking at it in this way reminds you that the moving average is very much a lagging indicator, simply showing the past.

As you might imagine, if you can change how many time periods you average together you can generate a whole family of moving average lines with different values, plotting a new position on each line each day.

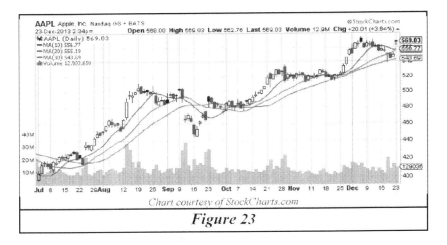

Chart courtesy of StockCharts.com

Figure 23

Figure 23 is the daily chart of Apple prices, with moving averages based on 10 days, 20 days, and 30 days. The line closest to the price is the 10 day line, next is the 20 day, and finally the 30 day. This is as you would expect, as the less number of days you take to average up, the closer the value will be to the current price.

You may not be able to see it on the scale of this chart, but the shorthand for the moving averages is shown in the top left – SMA(10), SMA(20), and SMA(30). SMA stands for Simple Moving Average, which means that these are calculated by adding together the prices and dividing by the number of prices.

As the moving averages are based on historic numbers, technical analysts have tried to make the more recent prices have more influence, bringing them closer to the current price movement. This means there are several other types of "average" which generally have bias to the latest numbers. The most common alternative is the exponential moving average (EMA), and you can experiment with the variations when you develop your analysis techniques.

It is conventional to base all these average calculations on the closing prices, but some technical analysts like to try alternates, such as the average of the high, low, open, and close prices. With most charting packages, you will be on your own if you want to pursue this, as you will not be able to alter what prices are used. In practice, the number of periods you decide to average usually has a much greater effect than the consideration of which price to use.

Single Moving Average

One of the most basic techniques for analyzing prices and making trades uses a single moving average line. You plot the line on the price chart, and when the price rises up above the moving average you enter a long trade. The price often keeps going up once it has risen above the moving average line, as you can see from the chart above.

If you choose an SMA(10), then you can expect to see frequent crossings, trade more often, and perhaps have false signals; if you choose a longer time, such as an SMA(50), then you will have less signals and less trading, not so many false signals, but may miss out on some moves.

As with all trading strategies, you need to experiment and find what works best for you and for the security you are trading.

We will talk about methods for closing trades later. You could simply close the trade if the price drops down below the moving average, or you could use a more sophisticated signal.

All these comments also apply if you are considering going short on a downtrend, when your signal would be the price dropping down below the moving average.

Two Moving Averages

The next level of sophistication you might look at for trading uses two moving averages of different periods. This is called the double crossover method. The signal to trade is when the moving averages cross each other.

You can choose from many different combinations of moving average. Look for instance at the SMA(10) and SMA(30) crossings above.

When the shorter-term moving average rises above the longer-term, this is a signal to trade long – it is a similar idea to the price rising above a moving average, but smoothed out as you are using averages for both. This prevents so many false signals.

You can see this system would have worked quite well on the chart above, with a long trade being entered early on the left-hand side. Whatever closing signal you used, you would probably get a decent profit from this. A trading signal happens again around the middle of the chart, and this again would be profitable in this example.

Once again you can use the same system if you want to go short, just invert the instructions.

Three Moving Averages

Somewhat inevitably, the next level of sophistication uses three moving averages, and is called the triple crossover method. Many times it is not worth complicating matters this much – no matter how sophisticated any method is, you will have a share of losers. Arguably, you are better off using a simple system that you know you can apply consistently.

The triple crossover method is used mostly in the futures market, and you can look on it as a development of the double crossover method that incorporates an additional confirmation of the trade. Common values used are SMA(4), SMA(9), and SMA(18), and sometimes 5, 10, and 20.

Suppose you are in a downtrend, and the SMA(4) rises above the other two moving averages. This would be a signal to close any short positions you may be in from previous action, and to watch out for a buying opportunity to come. When the SMA(9) goes above the SMA(18), this is a confirmation and you open a long trade.

Similarly, if you are in a long trade and the SMA(4) drops down below the other two moving averages, this is a signal to close your long trade. You wait until the SMA(9) drops below the SMA(18) before opening a short position.

Bollinger Bands

We will come back to discuss moving averages and other ways that they are used in trading strategies later on. For now, I want to introduce a charting feature closely related to moving averages. Bollinger Bands were invented by John Bollinger, and are based on a moving average, but with lines either side of it that in practice indicate the expected range of price movement. Figure 24 gives an example on the Apple chart.

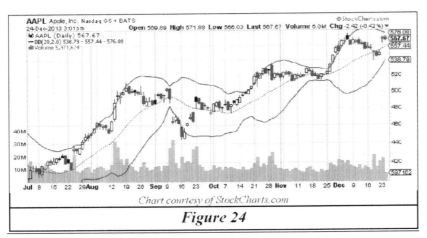

Chart courtesy of StockCharts.com

Figure 24

Once again all parameters are settable, but charting programs usually default to the commonly used ones, in this case "20" and "2". The "20" refers to the moving average, the middle line, which is an

SMA(20) line. The "2" sets how far away the outer lines are from the moving average.

The outer lines are drawn using a statistical calculation on how volatile the price is. The more volatile, or likely to fluctuate the price is, the wider the lines are. This means that they include about 95% of all the price movement, so the mathematicians tell us. In technical terms, the lines are set at 2 x the standard deviation from the moving average.

There are some interesting things that happen, when you draw these Bollinger Bands. First, in an uptrend you will see that the price tends to run along the upper band. The upper band provides some sort of target price for a trending stock.

In more general terms, you can expect the price in an uptrend to be in the area between the moving average and the upper band. If it drops below the moving average, then it is likely that the trend is changing.

The other thing you can see is that the bands narrow and get wider. Often when the bands narrow down, it is just before the price breaks out in one direction or another, and you can see examples of that in the chart. It is almost like the price is being throttled down until it cannot stand being contained anymore, so suddenly it goes on a run.

It occurs sufficiently frequently that you can expect to see a price break out after the Bollinger Bands narrow, giving you good warning of a tradable situation.

Optimizing the Numbers

I have mentioned a few numbers in connection with moving averages, and this is one place where you can experiment when you are trading, to see if different numbers produce better results.

The default numbers that you find on your charting program usually work fairly well, as they have a lot of history going into them – however you can refine the values, and run tests to see if they are any better. Usually if you reduce the number, shortening the period, you will find you have more trading signals.

It is doubtful if changing the number by one or two will produce any noticeable consistent improvement. If you want to look at how it would have performed in the past, this is done by "back testing", which is covered in the final chapter.

Bear in mind that moving averages naturally work better when there is a trend in the price, and are pretty well meaningless if there is no trend. As markets do not trend half the time, you must be careful when deciding to use moving averages to help your trading.

Technical Indicators

Technical indicators and oscillators are used in technical analysis to try and indicate the market sentiment, which in turn will suggest what may happen to the price in future. As technical as they get, you must always remember that none of them are guaranteed, and only give an indication of probability.

Oscillators are typically shown underneath the price chart, although they are sometimes superimposed in the price area. The chief point of an oscillator is that it indicates when the market is reaching an extreme condition, either overpriced, also called overbought, or underpriced which is known as oversold.

If the market is overbought, this shows that the price has gone up quickly and enthusiastically, and perhaps has reached a level higher than is sustainable. In other words, you might expect the price to fall back.

When the market is oversold, this implies that the market participants have rushed to unload their shares for whatever reason, and you may be able to pick up bargains in the expectation that the price will come back up when it stabilizes.

There are many different indicators, and I invite you to log into some charting software so that you can view them. You can go to one of the big financial sites such as those offered by MSN or Yahoo! or look at one of the many others available. In this book, I have used charts from **www.stockcharts.com**, whose copying conditions allow reproduction, provided it is attributed and referred back to their website. Simply go to their SharpCharts for a full range of controls.

You can find copies of all the charts and diagrams in this book on the associated website, **www.newbiesguidetotechnicalanalysis.com**, and you will be able to see the charts in color, which may make them easier to read.

Apart from indicating a change in market sentiment, oscillators can also be used to show when a trend is slowing down, often before this becomes obvious in the price chart. Despite the large number of indicators, most of them are used in a similar way, conforming to these general guidelines.

Before you feel overwhelmed at the sheer range of oscillators available, you need to know that traders do not refer to many of them in the general run of things. In fact, once you have a trading system defined you may find that you only need a couple of indicators on the chart.

Most everyone will tell you that you need to use at least two methods when identifying trading opportunities, so that you have some confirmation before staking your money. That does not mean that you have to use two indicators, as other factors can confirm.

The confirmation could be looking for a pattern or price breaking a support line, for example. But if you use more than one indicator, try to make sure that they are not based on the same type of information, such as momentum or volume, so that you have a more independent second view.

With all that said, we will now look at some of the most popular technical indicators.

Relative Strength Index (RSI)

The relative strength index was invented a few decades ago, and it compares a stock performance to itself over time.

The formula works by looking at the average up days and down days closing prices, and calculates the momentum of the market in either direction, which is plotted underneath the price chart. The values are usually normalized to be from 0 to 100, and boundary levels are drawn at 30% and 70%, as shown in Figure 25 overleaf.

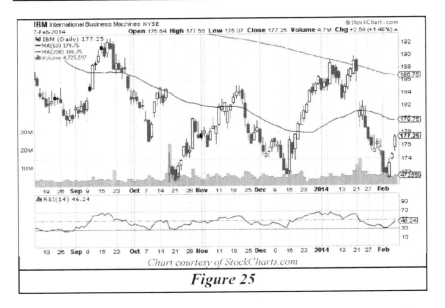

Figure 25

You do not necessarily trade when the value goes above 70% or below 30%, as a trend can still be quite strong. But when the value comes back towards the center past the boundary level, it is time to watch out for other signs that the trend is changing and to make a trade.

You can also see on this chart of IBM that the RSI does not necessarily reach 30% or 70% before turning back. It may be you would have to play with the values if you are trading this particular stock in order to make it more effective. The value of the indicator is that you can see when you have reached the effective end of the trend and started back, and this is not always obvious from simply observing the price, as the price chart does not have simple "boundary levels".

You can see another trait of indicators on this chart. Indicators always tend to follow the price level, giving a smaller version of the chart. Anytime the indicator line is going in the opposite direction to the price line, then you should watch out for changes.

Stochastic Oscillator

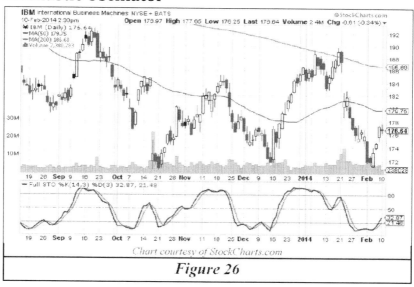

Figure 26

Figure 26 shows the stochastic oscillator, shown underneath the same IBM price chart. Note how the general form, the ups and downs, is similar to the previous indicator and the price line, as just mentioned.

This indicator was very popular in the 1990s, and is a little more complex in its treatment of price action than many others, which means it is often more effective.

The oscillator was invented by Dr. George Lane, who at the time of testing many different forms of indicator. If you look at the heading of the oscillator section, you will see %K and %D. This simply shows how far Lane had gone along in the alphabet before he came upon this particular calculation.

The initial idea is to look at where the closing price is in relation to the price bar. In an uptrend, the price will tend to close towards the top of the range, and in a downtrend the price will close towards the bottom. The oscillator sets a percentage to the position of the closing price in relation to the range.

That is actually reflected on %K, the black or darker line. %D is the lighter line which lags behind. It is actually a three day moving average of the %K, and it is used as a signal line when trading.

There are several ways you can use it, but a common one is to wait for a divergence between the two lines when they are in an overextended area, that is greater than 80% or less than 20%. Then when the lines cross, you have a signal to buy or sell, as appropriate.

Looking at the middle of the chart, you can see where the black line crosses down through the lighter line (just before Dec). As the lines are in the overbought area, above 80%, this is a sign to sell.

Moving Average Convergence/Divergence

While most of the indicators you can plot are similar to the previous two, the Moving Average Convergence/Divergence (MACD), which is also known as the "Mac Dee", is a bit more complicated, combining the oscillator with a crossover system. Here once again it is shown on a chart from **www.stockcharts.com**.

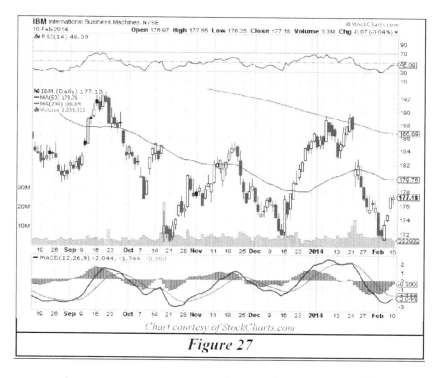

Figure 27

As you may guess from the name, the Mac Dee is based on moving averages, and attempts to take them at one stage further. It was invented by Gerald Appel.

It starts with two moving averages, a 12 day and 26 day in the default settings and in the example above. These are exponential moving averages, which as a reminder is a means of averaging prices to make them reflect more recent price action.

Now two moving averages can be combined on a chart, and where they cross is taken as a signal to buy or sell, as detailed in the previous chapter. The problem is that moving averages tend to lag behind what is happening now, so can give you a late signal.

What Appel did was plot the difference between the two averages, called the Mac Dee line. When the difference is zero, that is the same thing as the two averages crossing each other, but that does not tell you anything new although it does present the information in a different way.

But then Appel decided to show how much the difference was varying by plotting a moving average of the Mac Dee line. In this case it is a nine day exponential moving average, which now becomes a signal line which anticipates the crossing, and give an earlier signal.

The black or dark line is the Mac Dee line, the other is a signal line. When the black line crosses up through the signal line, and is in the lower section, that is a signal to buy. The opposite also applies.

Note that the Mac Dee also acts as an indicator which shows you overbought and oversold conditions. There are not any boundary levels drawn on, but if the Mac Dee is high the stock may be overbought, and if below the stock may be oversold.

As you can see, the Mac Dee also has a bar chart or histogram. This plots the difference between the two lines, so it gives you early warning if a trend is changing. If the histogram starts reducing or coming back to the middle zero line, then the trend is weakening.

Some people base their trading methodology mainly on the Mac Dee line, as it is a powerful tool and has various other ways that it can be interpreted.

Summary of Technical Indicators

There are many other indicators available, as you can easily see from any financial charting package. They go into and out of favor, but mainly are used in similar ways. You should try testing a few to see which you like as well as which work well on the financial instrument you intend trading.

The principles that apply almost universally to all oscillators are as follows: –

- The oscillator is most useful when it is at an extreme, either high or low. It can indicate that the price is overextended, but note it can reach an extreme in the early stages of a trend, so a reversal is more clearly indicated when the indicator starts coming back towards the center.

- If you see the price line and the oscillator going in different directions, then that is a transient situation and you should expect changes to come.

- You may also look for the oscillator to cross the zero or middle line as a signal. Generally, you will only want to buy long if the oscillator is below the middle, and to sell short if the oscillator is above zero.

- An oscillator is a secondary indicator, and you should always do a trend analysis, and not be tempted to trade against the trend simply because of the oscillator signal.

No matter which oscillators you decide to use, you can experiment with the variables to find those that seem to work best with the financial security you are trading. Some traders, for instance, try and relate the variables to market cycles.

Whether you try and relate them to cycles or not, remember that you can use exactly the same oscillators and indicators on any time scale chart. So if you are looking at a weekly or monthly chart to get an overall picture of where the security is going, feel free to add your favorite indicators and see what they will tell you.

Candlestick Charting

Candlestick charting was outlined in the Basic Charting chapter. Here is the diagram again:

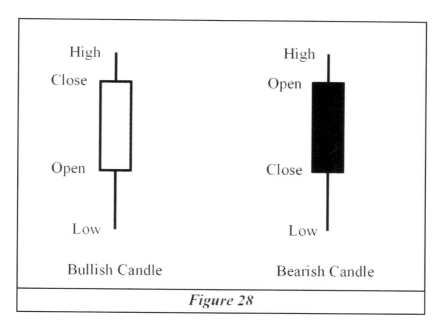

Figure 28

The solid part is the real body, and the lines above and below are called wicks or shadows. The color of the body clearly shows whether the price rose or fell over the day, from market opening to market closing.

Despite the fact that candlestick charts were only discovered in the Western trading world in the 1980s, they have been used by the Japanese for centuries. They provide a visual indication of market sentiment, provided you understand the principles of their interpretation.

Interpretation involves looking for patterns, and the patterns may consist of one or more candlesticks. Almost invariably you will need the pattern to occur in a particular trend for it to be meaningful. Candlestick patterns are usually identified before a trend reversal, and this is their main use; however, some patterns also indicate a continuation of a current trend.

The power of computers means that some charting software can be set to automatically point out common candlestick patterns. Although this is a useful facility, you need to confirm that the patterns are really relevant before relying on them.

Different Shapes

Figure 28 shows you a couple of typical candlesticks, but as you can imagine that there are many different variations, and each has been accorded some meaning. The length of the real body, the difference between the opening and closing prices, can vary from zero up to a theoretical unlimited length. Similarly, the wicks may be long, short, or nonexistent, and can be different on each end.

Doji

The first shape to look at is the "doji", a Japanese name. This has no length to the real body, which appears as a simple horizontal line. The opening and closing prices are exactly the same.

While the real body may have no length, the wicks can be any length. The Japanese regard the doji as very significant. This is because if both the opening and closing prices are the same, it stands to reason that the market is undecided and somewhat in balance. Therefore this candle will often occur when a trend is about to reverse. This is even more likely if there is a high trading volume on that day.

Spinning Top

Similar to the doji, the spinning top has a short real body. It usually has long upper and lower wicks – you can see the allusion to a spinning top. Once again, in general it may represent indecision, particularly if the body is significantly shorter than that of adjacent candles.

Long Body

If you have a candlestick with a particularly long body, then obviously this is the opposite of the indecision of the doji. It shows that there is a strong move in the market, with the closing price being very different from the opening price.

There is a special name for the long body candle which has no wicks. It is called a Marubozu.

It only occurs if the opening and closing prices are at the extreme values that were traded.

Reversal Patterns

The simplest patterns consist of one candlestick. As previously mentioned, it must occur in a trend to be significant. This is fairly obvious, as unless there is a trend there is nothing to be reversed.

Doji

The doji is available in various configurations, depending on the length of wicks. For instance, the dragonfly doji is a doji that has no upper wick, so both opening and closing prices are at the top, and are represented by a single horizontal line. Unless derived from the Japanese, quite often the names of candlestick patterns are descriptive, as in this case.

This pattern is often regarded as bullish, more so if you see it in a downtrend when you may see a trend reversal.

The complementary pattern to this is called the gravestone doji. It has the line for the real body at the base, and an upper wick. Again, a descriptive name. Most often a bearish signal, especially if you see it in a downtrend. The shape of the candlestick shows that the price has ranged up during the day, but the bullish traders could not keep it there. It drops back down by the close, which suggests the bulls are losing control.

The Hammer Family

I combine together four different single candle patterns in this section, as they are all similar in appearance and reasoning.

The Hammer

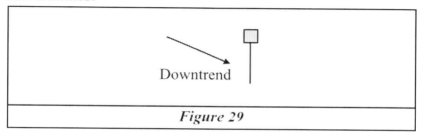

Figure 29

Figure 29 shows the classic Hammer candlestick. The color of the body does not matter, so I have left it grey. The lower shadow must be two or three times the length of the body, and the reversal signal is stronger the longer it is. After a Hammer, you can look for the trend to reverse and become bullish.

Once again, you can think through what the candle is telling you. In this case, there was trading at lower levels but the market was not prepared to let the stock finish up so cheaply, so the price came back up by the close. This suggests that the bears are not in control anymore.

The Hanging Man

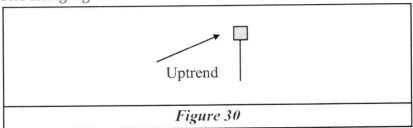

Figure 30

The hanging man (Figure 30) looks the same as the hammer, but occurs in an uptrend, and suggests a reversal to a downtrend. The theory behind it is that the market traded lower during the day, but the bears did not finish in control. If the stock is overbought, anyone with a short position may be buying to cover and that is what sustains the price. But anyone with a long position seeing the long range downwards would be thinking of selling while the price is still high, so the increase in supply will drive the price down in the next few days.

Imverted Hammer

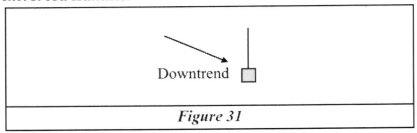

Figure 31

The same principle can be applied to the inverted hammer, which is considered a bullish signal. The bulls failed to control, but those with a short position may be getting worried. As you close a short position by buying, this pushes the price up in the following days.

Shooting Star

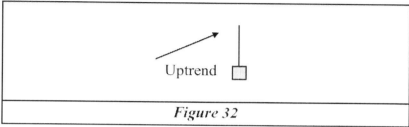

Uptrend

Figure 32

The fourth hammer-like candle, illustrated above, is called a shooting star, and the explanation takes us back to the original hammer. While the stock traded up during the day, it could not keep the price by the close and this suggests that the uptrend may be over. Once again, the pattern portends a reversal in trend.

Engulfing Patterns

Quite simply, the engulfing pattern is a two candle pattern where the second candle "engulfs" the first one by its sheer size. The second candle is a countertrend candle, so that gives a strong indication that the trend is going to change. Figure 33 (over) shows a Bullish Engulfing pattern.

With a strong bullish candle that totally engulfs the real body of the previous one, this suggests that the trend is about to turn upwards. The pattern is satisfied even if the shadows of the first candle are not engulfed.

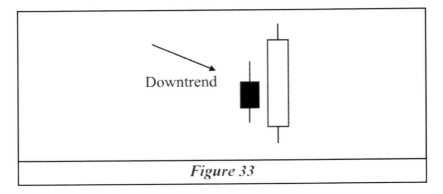

Figure 33

The Bearish Engulfing pattern in Figure 34 below follows a similar line of reasoning.

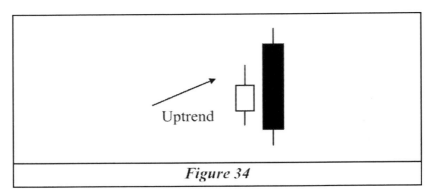

Figure 34

Harami

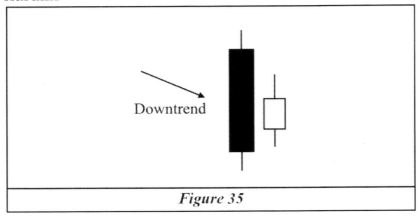

Figure 35

Harami, I understand, means "pregnant" in Japanese, and the Harami pattern looks like the profile of a pregnant woman. Once again, there are both bullish and bearish versions.

Figure 35 (previous page) shows a Bullish Harami. There is a different concept, or explanation, for why the Harami indicates a reversal. For the bullish harami, the first day is a long day in the downtrend. The second day starts higher, and goes countertrend, which suggests an underlying weakness. This may be accompanied with lower trading volume on the second day.

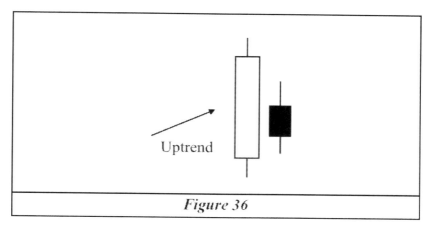

Figure 36

Figure 36 is a Bearish Harami. In the same way as the bullish, the first day is a long day in the existing uptrend. On the second day the price is not maintained for the opening, and sinks by the time the day is finished. Possibly the market is tired with the uptrend, so this is likely to result in a reversal to a downtrend.

Summary of Candlesticks

These are just a few of the many cataloged candlestick patterns, but they are the main ones. Most traders only use a few known ones. If you are interested in a full listing and more detailed explanations, I would recommend you check out my book, *"The Complete Guide To Candlestick Charting"*, which lists nearly 100 patterns.

There are a few principles that you need to bear in mind if you want to use candlestick patterns in your trading.

- Always use other trading tools such as Western charting analysis, in addition to candlesticks.

- Look for agreement between what the candlestick patterns tell you and what other trading tools tell you.

- To be valid, a candlestick pattern must not only be the right shape, but must occur in the correct trend.

- The candlestick pattern alone is not justification for trade.

If a doji sets a new high, wait for the next candle to close below the doji to confirm a bearish reversal.

Ichimoku Cloud Charts

As mentioned, candlestick charting was only discovered by Western traders in the 1980s, even though it had been known in Japan for a few centuries. It is not often that there is such a major breakthrough in technical analysis, but the recent discovery of another Japanese trading tool may be the next one.

The name of the tool in Japan is Ichimoku Kinko Hyo, and that translates to "at one glance balance bar chart". In the West it is either called Ichimoku, or more easily Cloud Charts. The Japanese trader Goichi Hosada discovered it in the 1930s, though only revealed it publicly in the 60s. It is still newly arrived to the Western trader.

The charts look a little more complex than regular price charts, which is ironic when you realize the translation is "at one glance". But once you get used to them, you will find that you quickly determine the information you need about the way a stock is trending. So that you can compare them, here is the previous candlestick chart and the comparable Ichimoku chart.

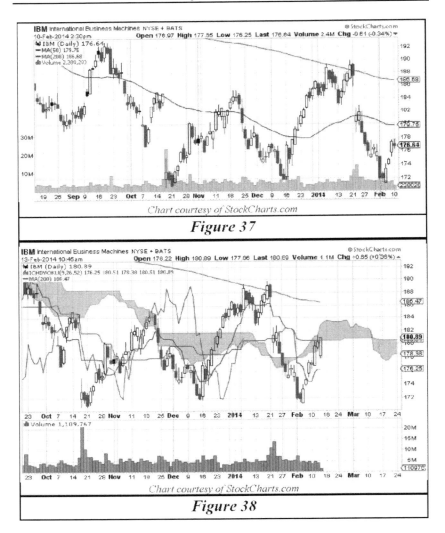

Chart courtesy of StockCharts.com

Figure 37

Chart courtesy of StockCharts.com

Figure 38

The first thing you will notice is that the Ichimoku chart is shifted along – that is because some of Ichimoku involves projecting ahead, and the chart shows all of it. These charts still come from **www.stockcharts.com**, where the Ichimoku elements come in under "Overlays".

Ichimoku involves colored elements, so you may find it easier to follow along if you look at the charts on the companion website, **www.newbiesguidetotechnicalanalysis.com**.

Conventional Western charting makes great use of moving averages. As I describe the elements of an Ichimoku chart, you will note that the Japanese in this instance favor using midpoints of the high and low levels. That is they take the highest level and the lowest level over the period of time and average them – similar to an average of all the points, but somewhat simpler, and probably easier to calculate when these charts were first developed in the 1930s.

There are in fact five different lines calculated to make an Ichimoku chart, though two of them are the boundaries to the cloud formation, and therefore not seen as separate lines.

Standard Line

The standard line, which may also be called the baseline, is the midpoint of the highest and lowest values for the last 26 days. Twenty six days equates to the number of trading days in a typical month, which may be why this was chosen originally. Therefore effectively this is a medium-term moving average.

Turning Line

The turning line, which can be called the conversion line, is similar but for only the last nine days. This period apparently comes from it being one and a half times the original six day trading week. Once again, you can look on this in terms of moving average lines, and it would be the fast average.

The difference between this method of line construction and true averages is that you will notice these lines can have spells where they are horizontal, that is the same value from day to day, simply because the highest and lowest values occurred fairly recently, and thus are used again and again on each successive day.

Cloud Lines

The two cloud lines are called the Cloud Span A and Cloud Span B, and this is where Ichimoku deviates most significantly from Western indicators.

Cloud Span A

The Cloud Span A line is the midpoint between the standard line and the turning line, but shifted forward 26 days. This action has never been done with Western indicators to my knowledge.

Cloud Span B

The Cloud Span B line is the midpoint between high and low values for the last 52 days, or two months, again shifted forward by 26 days, to line up with Cloud Span A.

Looking back at the chart, you can see how these lines which form the cloud boundaries are shifted forward 26 days, running into the future where the price has not gone yet.

Lagging Line

The fifth line mixes up easy and innovative. It is simply the closing price line, but the innovative part is that it is shifted back 26 sessions before plotting. So this line cannot even be drawn up to the present day, because it depends on future prices that are not yet known.

It will be easier for you to understand the distinct ways the Ichimoku chart is used if you can either pull up the charts on the website, or alternatively generate new ones to see how the lines work out. You will be able to choose different color combinations, so that you can distinguish the various features.

Now the Cloud Span A line is the midpoint between the 9 day line and the 26 day line, so you can think of it as a 17 1/2 day line, similar to a moving average. The Cloud Span B line is the 52 day midpoint, so think of it as a 52 day moving average.

Thinking back to moving averages, when the fast or short-term moving average is above the longer-term average, it counts as a bullish sign. In a similar way, when Cloud Span A line is over Cloud Span B line, this is also bullish – with the significant difference that it is shown 26 days in the future.

For the chart shown, the bullish cloud is colored green by **StockCharts.com**. Though drawn in the future, it is a reflection of the bullish trend that happened a few weeks ago. When the situation reverses and B is over A, the bearish cloud is shown in red.

When you start using cloud charts you should take some time to set the colors and thicknesses to values that are clear to you. This may also depend on what way you choose to use them, as you may want to highlight different features. Some people take the candlesticks off, leaving a simple price line for clarity, but I recommend you do not do this as you can obtain valuable information from candlestick patterns.

Interpretation

As you might expect, there are many ways that the different signals provided by the Ichimoku can be applied. One of the first things you may notice is how much impact the cloud seems to have on the price.

Often the cloud edges provide support or resistance, and this applies whether the price approaches from inside or outside the cloud.

When you glance at the chart, you will see that if the price is above the cloud it is usually an uptrend, and if the price is below you are frequently in a downtrend. If the price is inside the cloud, the situation usually needs watching, and the result may be the price crossing the cloud and changing trend, or finding support or resistance and going back.

The cloud itself is usually thicker in a good trend, and when it goes thinner the trend might be about to change.

Signals

The lagging line is used a lot for confirmations. When it crosses the cloud, this can be taken as confirming a change in trend. You may see a start to the trend changing when the price crosses, but the lagging line is more likely to be correct.

You will find that the cloud provides support and resistance not just to the price, but also to the lagging line. Either of these may run along the edge of the cloud.

The turning line and the standard line are considered very important by some experts, and can be interpreted in the same way as moving averages, as intimated above. This works particularly well if the price has drifted a long way from the cloud, as it may take time to come back and provide a signal. Looking for the turning line and standard line crossing will give you an earlier indication of the change in trend.

Having said that, other experts do not bother much with the turning line and standard line, and even take them off the chart to simplify matters. These different points of view simply serve to emphasize how new the study of the Ichimoku technique is, with no settled optimum interpretation.

There is much more to Ichimoku charts than I can include in this guide, so if you are interested in them I recommend picking up a copy of *Cloud Charts: Trading Success with the Ichimoku Technique* by David Beckett Linton. It is a worthwhile investment, complete with colored charts of excellent quality, and provides a comprehensive guide. I bought my copy as soon as it came out in 2010.

Elliott Waves and Fibonacci

E lliott Wave Theory was popularized in the 1970s, though Elliott first used his ideas in the 1930s. It builds on the Dow Theory, and basically describes price movement as a series of waves.

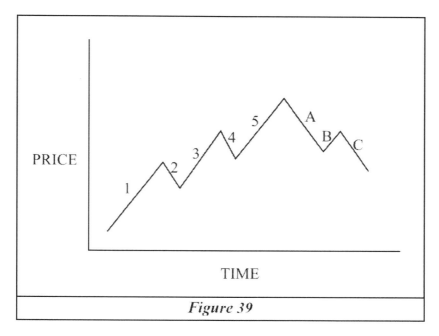

Figure 39

Elliott said that stock market prices tend to repeat a certain pattern, and that pattern is a five wave advance followed by a three wave decline, as shown in Figure 39, where wave is any price movement up or down.

The numbering and lettering is conventional. Waves 1, 3, and 5 are in the direction of the trend, and called impulsive waves, and waves 2 and 4 are retracements or corrections and called corrective waves.

Waves A, B, and C make up a retracement to the main trend 1 - 5. In this case, A and C are impulsive waves in the main direction of the move, and B is the corrective wave.

Taken as a whole, 1 - 5 can be regarded as a move in trend, and A - C as the retracement. If the trend continues, it should keep repeating this 5 – 3 pattern.

Actually, Elliott did not say that there would only be this form, the five wave pattern, but that idea was put forward by his followers in the 1970s, so is the generally accepted standard.

So far so good, but not terribly interesting. The key to the fascination and complexity of Elliott Waves is that this process is scalable, both up and down.

For example, this initial 5 – 3 pattern can be subdivided into smaller waves, with wave 1 becoming five smaller waves and wave 2 becoming three smaller waves to make the same kind of wave pattern. Doing this for all the original waves, you come up with Figure 40.

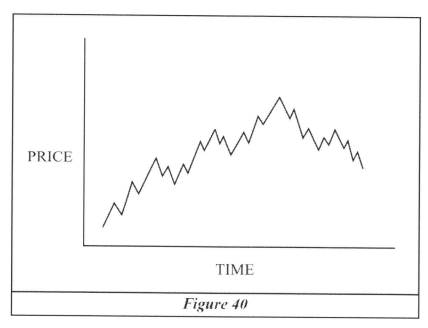

Figure 40

And so on...

The original pattern can also be viewed as the first two waves of a larger pattern. Elliott invented names for the size of each pattern, from a Grand Supercycle which might last for a century or more to a Subminuette which might only last a few minutes. The names do not matter for the sake of knowing about Elliott Waves.

To some extent, I find Elliott Waves far more convincing in retrospect, when you can fit the price moves into the form you want, than when used for prediction. However, many people are passionate about Elliott Waves, with books, magazines, and societies developing the ideas, so it seems there is something to it.

If you are interested in pursuing the study of Elliott Waves, there is plenty of specialist information available. For the sake of acquaintanceship with the principles, you can start by studying these basic rules or guidelines: –

- Corrections never have five waves. If it appears a correction has five waves it is likely the first wave of a much larger three wave decline. Alternatively, it may be the start of a trend in the other direction.

- The basic cycle is not complete until you see both the five wave and three wave patterns.

- Wave three of the five waves is never the shortest, and usually the longest.

- Looking at the impulsive waves 1, 3, and 5, often two will be equal in length, and these are usually 1 and 5.

- Looking at the corrective waves 2 and 4, they usually tend to be equal in length, too.

- Often the length of 1 and 4 is the same.

- Often the length of 2 and 5 is the same.

- The lowest point of wave 4 must never be lower than the lowest point of wave 2. If it is, you have wrongly interpreted the pattern.

- For the three wave correction, often waves A and C will be equal.

- The three wave correction typically retraces about one third of the five wave movement. Look for it to stop at the level of wave 4's lowest point.

Experts have analyzed and produced other ideas for wave patterns which are gone into in considerable depth in the literature. Whether you can use such things to improve your trading depends on how you see the patterns.

Fibonacci Numbers

Fibonacci was an Italian who lived in the 13th century, and he discovered the Fibonacci series of numbers, which is formed by adding together the previous two numbers to make the next. The start of the series is 1, 1, 2, 3, 5, 8, 13, 21, 34, 55, 89, 144, 233, etc.

There are many intriguing properties to this series. Elliott said in his book "Nature's Law" that the wave principle was based on the Fibonacci sequence. As you subdivide down waves, the

Fibonacci series describes how many waves overall you have.

The series tends towards a fixed ratio between adjacent numbers, and the ratio is 1.0:1.618 approximately. This ratio is also 0.618:1.0, that is 1.618-1.0:1.0.

Elliott put together some more guidelines which referred to this Fibonacci number: –

- The length of wave 3 is often wave 1 multiplied by 1.618.

- You can find the target for the top of wave 5 by multiplying wave 1 by 1.618, and doubling it. The top of wave five will be between this value and this value plus the length of wave 1.

- For the three wave correction where wave A and wave C are equal, wave C is 0.618 times the length of wave A below the bottom of wave A.

You can see how this topic can rapidly become complex and needs treatment in a separate volume.

Fibonacci Retracements

Even if you are put off by the complexity of Elliott Waves – and it is not necessary to consult them if you choose to use one of the many other methods of technical analysis – you may find the Fibonacci number of much greater use.

Traders use the value of 61.8% and its complement 38.2%, in round terms 62% and 38%, as target levels for anticipating support and resistances and predicting the depth of retracements. Although not Fibonacci, 50% is usually added too.

Most charting software allows you to pull out a set of parallel lines using a mouse, with these percentage relationships. Generally, you can pull the lines out between a low point and a high point, and will see the support and resistance effects of the levels. Superimposing these on the previous IBM chart gives Figure 41.

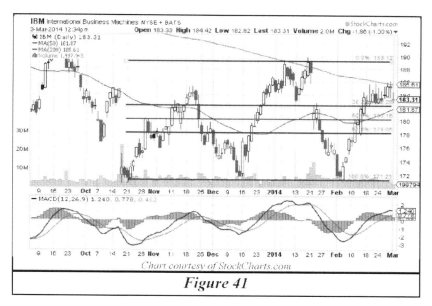

Figure 41

(As before, you can look on the website for clarity and to see the colors)

The Fibonacci lines are pulled out between the low point in the middle and the high point about three quarters of the way across. The various relationships to the lines are obvious. The 38% (upper) line in particular figures as support and resistance several times.

You are not restricted to pulling out the Fibonacci levels between the lowest and highest points, but can use any significant price levels. If you try it for yourself, you will be surprised how often the Fibonacci lines seem to fall in significant places.

Money Management

If you want to learn technical analysis, you are obviously thinking of trading on the financial markets. While it is not strictly technical analysis, this chapter on money management is important for anyone contemplating trading.

No one has yet come up with a computer program that you can simply set going, and sit back reaping in profits. While it is possible to automate many of the things we have looked at, uncertainty is at the heart of trading, and how you deal with that uncertainty determines whether you will succeed.

Money management is all about how you allocate your money into the different trades that you select. Technical analysis gives you pointers on which trades are worth picking, but it cannot control your overall plan.

Picking the right entry and exit points is reckoned to account for only 10% of trading. Money management is responsible for 30%, and psychology covers the remaining 60%, showing just how difficult it can be mentally to make a success of it.

Guidelines

Here are some guidelines that you might like to adopt at the outset of your trading. They have been developed over the years, and are designed to minimize the amount of trouble you may get into. Once you are experienced, you can modify them, but I advise you to develop an understanding of why and how they are needed before making changes.

Limit your potential loss on any one trade to 2% of your trading account, updating this value as necessary. Depending what you trade, this does not mean you only use 2% of your account, simply that that is the maximum that you reasonably expect to lose if the trade does not work out.

Even then, limit the amount of your funds that you put on any one stock or financial instrument to 10% of your account, regardless of how good you think the trade is.

If you are putting several trades in the same market sector, try to limit your commitment to 25% of your account, as securities in a particular sector tend to move together.

If you are trading something where there may be a margin call, such as futures, do not commit more than 50% of your trading account to active trades so you have a reserve to fall back on, and do not have a high risk of a margin call.

Despite what you might think, your main aim when trading should not be to make a profit. Having this aim is likely to cloud your judgment. Your aim should be to trade well, and to preserve your capital. If you trade well, then the profit will come.

Diversification

As mentioned above, similar securities tend to move together and you should keep diversified in what you trade. It is even better if you have trades in securities that are traditionally negatively correlated, that is when one goes up the other goes down.

You might object that this prevents you making the maximum profit, which you would get if you put all your funds on the best performer. I would point out that you are not going to pick the best performer consistently, if ever, and should settle for what you can get with less risk.

Stoplosses

Every time you trade you need to have a stoploss level in mind. This is the level when you know the trade is not working out, and you need to exit to prevent losing any more funds.

As noted later, this can be set with your dealer, so that you do not have to keep watching the prices. Some people object to this practice, claiming that there can be price manipulation against you in some forms of trading.

This might seem like paranoia, but it is up to you. Just make sure you know the level of price at which you will close the trade and accept your losses.

Risk vs. Reward

Whenever you trade you should also have a good idea how much profit you may make. Knowing the amount of loss that you could suffer as well as the potential profit, you can work out the risk/reward ratio, which is how much you stand to lose versus how much you stand to gain.

Many traders say you need at least a 1 to 2 ratio, so that your winnings would be twice as much as what you might lose. Some say 1 to 3 ratio. The idea is that even if you only make winning trades half the time, having the advantage of this ratio you will still make a profit.

Position Sizing

Finally, working out the size of trades that you take is called position sizing. This is where you can relate the advice to not lose more than 2% of your account and your stoploss level and decide on how much to spend on any particular trade. Even if you are trading something which is not so straightforward as stocks, you can work out the potential loss for the amount you stake, and make sure it falls within bounds.

Types of Order

There are several different types of order or instruction you can give to your broker or dealer. Some of these depend on what type of security you are trading, but the main ones are generally available.

Market Order

This tells your broker to go and buy or sell on the market, getting the best price for you that he can consistent with doing it straightaway.

Limit Order

This tells your broker to go on to the market and buy or sell, as you instructed, provided he can do so for the price you ask or better. This means that the order may be delayed, depending how the market price varies.

The order might say "Go and buy XYZ shares with a limit of $30". If they are currently trading at $29, then the broker will get them at that price for you. If they are currently trading at $31, then the broker will watch the price to see if it comes down to $30 before he buys the shares for you.

Of course they may never come down to $30, in which case you will never buy the shares – but at least you will not have paid more than you wanted to.

You can modify this order by saying it is good for today only, so if the price does not come down today allowing the shares to be bought, then the order goes away; or you can say it is good till canceled (GTC) which means the broker will keep trying day after day to buy the shares at your price.

The same idea applies if you are selling, except your shares will not be sold unless the price is at least as high as your limit level.

Stop Order

There are several types of stop order. I have already mentioned the stoploss order, which tells your broker to sell your position at a certain level if the price goes against you, and I recommend that you use this whenever you open a new position, so that you are not caught out.

You can also use stop orders for buying and selling shares, and the effect is the opposite of the limit order. In other words, you will only buy the shares if the price goes up to a certain level, or sell the shares if the price goes down to a certain level. While that may sound strange, this might be useful if you want to buy the shares, but only if they start going up, for instance.

Trailing Stop

This is offered by most brokers, and is very useful to make sure that most of the profit you make is captured, even if the price comes back down.

In effect, it is a stop loss order with a varying price. The price level comes up as the price of the stock goes up, and keeps a certain distance from the price. The stoploss level never goes down, so if the price later goes down, it may hit the stoploss order, and your trade will be closed with the amount of profit that represents.

Similarly, if you have gone short on the trade, the trailing stop will follow the price down, making sure that you keep some of your gains even if the price comes back up, as the trailing stop will never go up again.

There are a few other orders which are not used much, and which may not be offered by all brokers. The ones given above will cover 99% of your needs.

Putting It Together

The purpose of studying technical analysis is to be more knowledgeable when it comes to trading, and to be able to develop ways or systems that are more likely to generate profit for you. Therefore this final chapter will talk about developing a trading system using your technical analysis skills.

Remember that you cannot expect the system to score highly all the time. You need to keep the ideas simple, so that you are able to use them freely, and not try to "fine tune" for the ultimate gains. Given the fickleness of the markets, this is mostly a waste of time and will only frustrate you.

You can purchase ready-made trading systems, and they can form a good basis for your own plan. If you do buy one, you may be surprised how obvious and straightforward it is. I think it is important that you review and modify it to your own needs. You need to take ownership in the plan so that you have confidence enough to stick with it regardless of recent results – there will be losing streaks that can make you try and second-guess what you are doing.

Your plan should preferably not leave any decisions to your discretion, but describe the action you take in all circumstances. This is for two reasons. First, you want whatever you do to be repeatable so that you can improve it and fix things if they do not work, without any subjective influences. Second, it will be easier to back test against historical data to make sure it is a winning strategy.

There are really only three questions to answer with your trading plan: –

1. Under what conditions will you enter a trade?
2. How much will you put in the trade?
3. Under what circumstances will you exit the trade?

Bearing this in mind, you can keep your trading plan simple and so make it easier to follow and implement.

Making an Entry

First let us say that this is not as critical as many people think. Use common sense to find a decent system, and just use it.

Van Tharp in his book, *Trade Your Way to Financial Freedom*, summarized the results of a random entry trading system. The entries were chosen at random, and whether the trade was long or short was chosen at random. There was a simple

1% risk money management system which was applied rigorously. The trading made money.

While it might not have made as much as you would hope to, if you can make money with random entries you can see why I ask you not to get too worried about how you find your entries.

You can choose to use a trend following system, as many traders do. Typically for this you will plot a long-term moving average, which will show you if and how the security is trending overall. Alternatively, you could look for a security that is trading at a new high, as this would indicate that the trend is upwards. Your signal to enter a trade may be from a single or double crossover method, or from one of the indicators.

Instead of trend following, perhaps you want to look for counter trend movement. This has a lower percentage chance of success, but the additional gains from identifying a new trend early can compensate. In this case, indicators can be a good reference for the market sentiment, and you can look for an approach to a strong support or resistance, ready to pounce at the first sign of a reversal. Candlestick patterns can give appropriate confirmation and timing.

However you choose an entry position, you should check that the trade represents a worthwhile risk before placing it. As mentioned previously, you want a risk/return ratio of 1:2 or better. With some systems, you may not have a definite target in mind, as you hope for the trend to continue for some time. Just be sure that the price charts show this is reasonable, and you do not for example have a strong resistance ahead that would curtail your gains.

Position Sizing

This topic was mentioned in the previous chapter on money management. The emphasis should be on preserving your trading capital, and not on risking more in the hope of greater gains. You need to work out your exit strategy for a losing trade so that you can work back to the size of stake.

The guideline that is recommended is risking losing no more than 2% of your trading account, though some professional traders regard even this as too chancy. Also be very careful that you do not commit too much of your account to several trades that may move together, and thus accumulate a much greater loss than planned. Reckon on a maximum of 10% of your account going into any particular financial security.

When to Exit

Closing out a trade can be one of the most difficult tasks for an inexperienced trader. This is not only because you have to identify the right price to do it at, but also because psychologically it can be extremely hard to close a losing trade in a timely manner.

There are two possible results for a trade. You win some, or you lose some. Your trading system has to cover both and do so efficiently, which means you minimize your losses if the trade goes against you and you maximize your gains if you are in profit.

The easiest way to contain your losses at the outset is to set a stop loss order. If you do not use this, you may find it difficult to close the trade when you should. The tendency is to wait and see if a losing trade turns around. After all, you put time and effort into finding what you thought would be a winning trade, so it is hard to dismiss it, and bruises your ego.

You have to learn to ignore this natural impulse if you do not use a stoploss, even though sometimes the trade will turn around after you have exited for a loss. That is just the nature of trading.

Your stoploss can be set a certain distance below your trade entry. You can set the distance by looking at how much the price has fluctuated in the last few weeks, or you can use technical analysis and the Average True Range (ATR) indicator for a more scientific solution. Typically, you might set the stop loss two times the ATR below the entry level.

Once a trade is starting to move in the right direction, it is a good plan to put a trailing stop order on, so if it reverses while you are not watching you will keep most of your gains.

Some traders advocate setting a profit target from the risk/return considerations, and placing an order to exit the trade when this value is reached. In many circumstances this may reduce the potential profit, so if you decide to use this you should make sure that this is what you really want to do for your particular trading strategy. It might be appropriate if you are taking regular gains from the fluctuations in range trading, as you expect the movement to be limited, but you would risk missing out on some of a move if you are trend following.

Back Testing

When you have completed the task of deciding on your entries, your position sizing, and your exits, it is time to see how effective they may be in the market. Certainly, you will have based your trading strategy on common wisdoms about the action of price and indicators, but you need to have the reassurance that what you have produced is going to be effective.

One way to do this is by a process called back testing, where you program a computer to apply your strategy to historic data, and see how well it would have performed. Provided your trading strategies allow, this is a good way to build confidence in your system, and therefore be more committed to follow it through thick and thin. Remember if you are tempted to change your system while you are actively trading, the chances are that your instincts and emotions will let you down. Your strategies should only be changed after deliberation, if really necessary.

There are many different ways to run a back test. MetaTrader is widely used, particularly for Forex trading, and has extensive back testing facilities and a great deal of user support and information. Other software such as Amibroker is competitively priced and has back testing facilities.

You can also manually back test any trading strategy, even though this may be long-winded. The advantages that you may get a better feel for how it works, and even think of improvements as you go along.

The purpose of back testing is twofold. I have already mentioned that you need to develop confidence in your system, so that you will follow it when trading, and therefore get the desired result. The other thing you can do is adjust any parameters that you are using, such as number of days in a moving average, to try and improve on your initial approach.

You should be wary of trying to optimize the parameters, and not get obsessive in fine-tuning them, but you may find some improvements can be made. For this reason, you should not use all your historical data when you first set up the back test. Instead, tweak the system using half the data, and run the test again using the other half to confirm that the strategy is still working.

The back test will give you a lot of information. You do not want to simply look at the bottom line, and accept the performance on this basis.

One of the factors you need to look at is the amount of drawdown you can expect. This is how much your account may be depleted during the course of trading. A high risk high profit strategy could for instance see times when your account is reduced by 50%, and unless you are prepared for and accept this it could well cause you some concern. I would expect there to be other issues in using such a strategy so it would be rejected, but you need the information that testing can give you.

Another statistic you might want to review is the percentage of wins you get versus the percentage of losses. I have already mentioned that you can have the same number or less wins, and still make a profit provided your risk/reward ratio is favorable. You need to compare the value of the wins to the cost of your losses.

One thing that is not always considered when looking at a new strategy is how many trades your system will require you to take, and compare this to your expectation and available time. If the strategy puts forward too many trades, you may be unable to keep up and find you are choosing between them, which will obviously be risky. On the other hand, if the strategy gives you too few opportunities, you might find that your capital is underutilized.

Paper Trading

Once you have your trading strategy sorted out, it can still be useful to test it out with "paper trading" before you commit any real money. Nowadays, paper trading is often done online rather than on paper, as most brokers will allow you to open a demo account which involves no money.

Some people dismiss paper trading as ineffective, because it is hard to have the same emotional reaction, which means you may act differently once you have money on the line. However, when you paper trade you will go through the motions, become familiar with implementing your strategy, and be able to see how the dealing software works.

Trading Journal

Finally, it is important that you keep a trading journal or diary as a record of trades. Apart from the obvious information, such as the security, the price, the profit or loss, etc., you should get in the habit of writing down your emotional state and the specific reasons that you entered and exited the trade.

If you can keep a full record of your actions, including printouts of the charts if relevant, this gives you valuable information and feedback so that you can continue to improve. I encourage you not to change your strategies too quickly, but perhaps review once a week to see what you might have done differently.

Further Reading

A couple of years ago I collaborated with others on the production of a detailed technical analysis course, designed to sell for a couple of thousand dollars. The course was based around a number of written modules that I produced, totaling about 100,000 words, and included related videos and online webinars.

While there is a market for these high end products, I recognize that many people cannot commit that expenditure, so I decided to release the written work, updated into book form, at a much lower price point. The book is called "*Mastering Technical Analysis*", and contains all the information. The videos were supplementary and covered selected items only.

At the time of writing this Newbies' Guide, the work is being updated and finally edited, but should be available shortly. Once again, there will be an associated website, and that is **www.masteringtechnicalanalysis.com**. To make the book affordable to the widest possible audience, I plan to price it well under a hundred dollars, but have not finalized the price yet.

If you want to be kept in touch with progress, please contact me at **alannorthcott@msn.com** or simply go to the website, which I will keep updated with progress.

About the Author

Alan Northcott has been writing and educating in the financial sector for many years and now resides in Florida. In addition to works published in his own name, Northcott has been responsible for the production of several trading courses, e-books and countless articles.

Also in this Newbies Series

_Forex - A Newbies Guide

"For anyone who's even thought about Forex and didn't know where to start, I can't imagine any newbie Forex book being more helpful than this. The author doesn't talk down to you, and he uses analogies that convey the concepts quickly and completely." – Aisling D'Art

Options Trading – A Newbies Guide

"Alan's Newbies Guide breaks down options trading to the newbie level in an easy to understand and follow style." – Usiere

Stocks – A Newbies Guide

"This is a great book to get a foot in the door and understand the basic concepts of stock investing." – Carlos Velez

Other Titles by This Author
The Complete Guide to Investing in Short Term Trading

The Complete Guide to Using Candlestick Charting

The Complete Guide to Investing in Gold and Precious Metals

The Complete Guide to Investing in Derivatives

The Complete Guide to Making Environmentally Friendly Investment Decisions

The Complete Guide to Investing in Real Estate Tax Liens & Deeds

The Mutual Funds Book

The Hedge Funds Book

Asset Protection for Business Owners and High Income Earners

Everything You Need to Know About Asset Allocation

For full reviews, see book listings on **www.amazon.com**.

Final Note

For an individual self-publishing, getting exposure in the market place in competition with the publishing big boys is one of the key challenges; but it is also one where you as a reader can help me enormously by spreading the word.

So, if you have enjoyed this book please help me to promote it by leaving a short review on Amazon. If you have any questions or problems, please drop me a line at **AlanNorthcott@MSN.com** and let me know, and I will do my best to answer them as well as revise the contents if necessary.

There is a wide range of ways you can help me including:

- Recommending the book to your friends;
- Posting a review on Amazon or other book websites;
- Reviewing it on your blog;
- Tweeting about it and giving a link to the website or to my author site at **www.alannorthcott.com**;
- Posting a link on your Facebook page

- Linking to my Facebook page or to my Linkedin profile;
- Following me on Twitter;
- Pinning it at Pinterest; or
- Anything else that you think of!

And if you would like to be kept in touch with each new book in the Newbies series, or if you have any other comments, please contact me at **alannorthcott@msn.com**

Many thanks for your help – it is much appreciated.

Alan Northcott

Made in the USA
San Bernardino, CA
11 January 2016